Feeling Your Way

DISCOVER YOUR SENSE
OF

VICKI COBB
Illustrations by
Cynthia C. Lewis

The Millbrook Press Brookfield, Connecticut

The author gratefully acknowledges Dr. Carl Sherrick, Senior Research Psychologist (Ret.) of the Cutaneous Laboratory, Princeton University, for his review of the manuscript and three amazing illusions. The author takes full responsibility for the accuracy of the text.

Published by The Millbrook Press, Inc.
2 Old New Milford Road
Brookfield, CT   06804
www.millbrookpress.com

Library of Congress Cataloging-in-Publication Data
Cobb, Vicki.
Feeling your way : discover your sense of touch / Vicki Cobb ;
illustrations by Cynthia C. Lewis.
p. cm. — (Five senses)
ISBN 0-7613-1657-4 (lib. bdg.) — ISBN 0-7613-1980-8 (pbk.)
1. Touch—Juvenile literature. [1. Touch. 2. Senses and sensation.]
I. Lewis, Cynthia Copeland, 1960– ill. II. Title.
QP451.C73 2001
612.8'8—dc21   00-032916

Close your eyes and feel this book.
Can you tell when your fingers are on this page?
Does this page feel different from the cover? How
do the edges of the pages feel compared to the surface?

Play a game with a friend. Close your eyes so that you can concentrate on your sense of touch. Have your friend put your fingers on different objects: an orange, an apple, a spoon, a sweater. Can you tell what the objects are just by feeling them? You bet! Your sense of touch, especially through your fingertips, can tell you a lot. Now try feeling the same things with your elbow. Can you tell if something is hot or cold or rough or smooth with your elbow skin?

You get enormous amounts of information about objects when you feel them with your hands. But you don't feel just

(Be sure to play the game with a friend who has a good sense of touch.

with your hands. You feel the wind on your face, the sun on your back, pebbles under your bare feet. Pain is an unpleasant and uncomfortable sensation. But it is important for warning you of dangers. Touches like hugs, pats on the back, shaking hands, and holding hands connect you with others. If infants

"The Princess and the Pea"

are not touched and held, they may find it difficult to have loving relationships in later life.

Scientists study our sense of touch by asking questions that can be answered by experiments. Some of these questions are: What is the lightest touch we can feel? Where is the most sensitive part of our body? How can our sense of touch be fooled? In this book, you are the scientist. Experiment to get in touch with your sense of touch!

How Touchy Are You?

WHAT TO DO WITH THE CARDBOARD TEETH AFTER YOU'VE DONE THE EXPERIMENT

Give it to someone with very little hair.

Hide it in someone's bed so they think a cat is sleeping under the covers.

Scare your friends and neighbors by pretending to be a vampire.

Discover how sensitive your sense of touch is.

Cut a piece of cardboard to make two triangular "teeth." The points of the teeth should be 3/4 inch apart.

Place the two teeth on your left cheek. Slowly drag the two teeth down your cheek and across your mouth. One point should be above your mouth and the other below it. Keep dragging them up your right cheek. Amazingly you will feel only one point on your left cheek that will become two and appear to spread apart as you pass over your mouth. The points seem to come together again on your right cheek. Clearly, your skin is much more sensitive around your mouth than on your cheeks!

What's the lightest touch you can feel, and where do you feel it? Cut a single hair about two inches long off a paintbrush. Close your eyes. Have a friend say "Ready? Now," just before touching you with the end of the hair. The hair should be pressed just hard enough to bend it slightly. Test different parts of your body. Can you always tell when the hair is touching you? Are some parts of your body more sensitive than others? The skin of the fingertips, lips, and tongue are the most sensitive. The least sensitive is the back of the leg.

Hitting a Nerve

Your skin is the organ for your sense of touch. The surface of your skin is a layer of dead cells that protect your insides from germs, poisons, and dirt from the outside world. If you put some tape on your skin and rip it off, you can see the dead skin cells sticking to the tape. Layers of living cells are under the

layer of dead cells. As the dead cells wear off, the living cells die and replace them.

Nerves that are part of your sense of touch are in these living layers. The parts of the nerves that respond to a touch are called receptors. Your receptors are connected by nerve fibers to your brain. The fibers are like telephone wires. Pressure, pain, heat, and cold make your nerves fire and send a message up to your brain. Only when your brain gets the message do you feel a touch.

A Race to the Brain

How long does it take a message from a receptor to reach your brain? It happens very fast. Would you believe as fast as 90 miles per hour? That's about half the length of a football field in one second! It's way too fast to measure without special instruments. But you can do an experiment and discover which touch will win a race to the brain.

Close your eyes and tap the tip of your index finger against your lip. Take off your shoe and sock and tap your finger on your little toe. Tap your two index fingers together.

If you are like most people, you will feel the taps more on your lip than on your finger, more on your finger than on your toe, and equally on both fingers. Since your two index fingers are equal distances from the brain, the race to the brain is a tie. The lip, however, is closer to the brain than your fingertip. So the message from the lip arrives a fraction of a second sooner and you feel the sensation more strongly on the lip. Your little toe, of course, is much farther from your brain than your finger. So your finger feels your toe more strongly than your toe feels your finger.

Feeling Double

You can fool your sense of touch. Put your index finger next to your middle finger. Touch the eraser end of a pencil to the groove between the fingers so that the pencil is touching both fingers at the same time. Close your eyes. You will feel the eraser as it really is—a single object.

Now cross your middle finger on top of your index finger. Put the pencil eraser on the surfaces of both fingers where they cross. Close your eyes and rub the eraser back and forth over the groove between your fingers. You will feel two erasers! If you rub the tip of your nose with your crossed fingers, it will feel as if you have two noses.

This happens because of the way your nerves are wired. You are accustomed to touching objects with your fingers uncrossed. The nerves from the touching sides of both fingers in this position go to the same part of the brain. The nerves from the outsides of each finger, however, do not normally touch a single object at the same time. So these nerves go to different parts of your brain. When you cross your fingers and touch an object to the two outsides of your fingers, your brain interprets the feeling as if there are two objects, not one.

Cool or Not Cool?

Both hands can be in the same bowl of water, yet one hand will feel cool and the other warm. Strange but true. See for yourself. You will need three bowls of water—one filled with hot water, one filled with cold water, and a third filled with room-temperature water. Put one hand in the hot water and the other in the cold water long enough for you to stop noticing how hot or cold the water is, two or three minutes. Then plunge both hands into the water at room temperature. Amazingly, the hand that was in hot water now feels cool, and the hand that was in cold water now feels warm.

Goldilocks ruins The Three Bears' experiment

"mmmM"

too HOT

too COld

Just Right

The reason is that your hot and cold receptors adapt. The receptors get tired and no longer fire messages to the brain. When you plunge both hands into the water at room temperature, different nerves fire in each hand. The hand that was in hot water now feels coolness, and the hand that was in cold water feels warmth. You've probably noticed temperature adaptation when you go swimming or take a bath. A pool feels cold when you first jump in, or a bath might feel too hot. But after a few minutes you don't notice the temperature anymore.

Now You Feel It, Now You Don't

Temperature is not the only sensation your nerves adapt to. Pressure is another one. You may notice the pressure from your belt or shoes when you get dressed in the morning. After a while the sensations disappear and you are no longer aware of them. Here's an experiment you can do with a friend to measure how your sense of pressure adapts.

Trace a quarter and the bottom of a soup can on a piece of cardboard. Cut out the two circles. Lie on your stomach and have a friend put the smaller circle on the skin of your back. Count the seconds (one-thousand one, one-thousand two, one-thousand three, and so on) until you no longer feel the cardboard. Do the same thing with the larger piece of cardboard. Which sensation disappears faster? Do the experiment again, but this time have your friend press lightly on each piece of cardboard.

A scientist who did this experiment found that you adapt faster to the larger piece of cardboard. But adding weight by pressing slows down adaptation. Do your results agree with this?

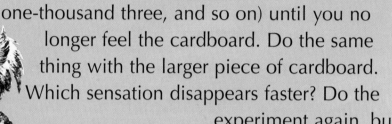

Soon, the sensation disappeared, and Harold forgot he had a monkey on his head.

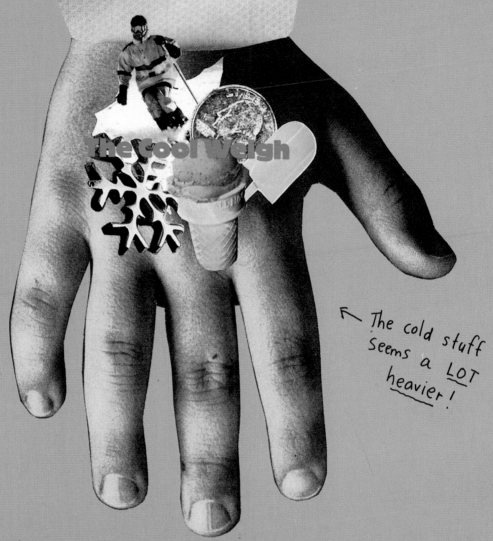

The cold stuff seems a LOT heavier!

Does the temperature of an object change the way you feel its pressure? Try this experiment to find out. Put a quarter in the refrigerator (not the freezer) for about three minutes. Put another quarter in some hot water at the same time. Put the cold quarter on the back of your hand. Make a mental note of how heavy it is. Replace the cold coin with the warm one. Does it seem heavier or lighter? Most people are surprised to find the cold coin seems a lot heavier. What happens when both coins are the same temperature as your skin?

Here's something else you can try with hot and cold quarters. Place a warm coin on the back of your hand or arm, and place a cold coin a couple of inches away from it. Within seconds you'll notice a definite sensation of cold underneath the warm coin. When you feel a temperature without any pressure, it's hard to know just where you're feeling it. If you feel pressure along with temperature, you feel the temperature at the point where you feel pressure. The sensation of cold seems to move under the pressure from the first coin. No one knows why this happens. It's a mystery scientists are still trying to figure out.

MYSTERIES SCIENTISTS ARE STILL TRYING TO FIGURE OUT

The warm coin/cold coin temperature-pressure thing

where the white goes when the snow melts

why we need "ph" when we already have a perfectly good letter "f"

how come a 10-minute punishment seems so much l-o-n-g-e-r than a 10-minute recess

why the same lunch tastes better out of a frog lunch box than out of a brown paper bag

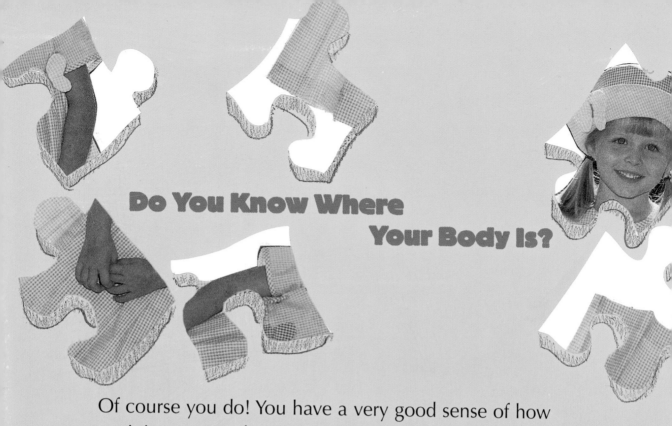

Do You Know Where Your Body Is?

Of course you do! You have a very good sense of how you are sitting, or standing, or moving around. That's because there are nerves going to all your muscles. The sense that tells you your body positions and movements is called *kinesthesis* (kin-es-THEE-sis), meaning "feeling motion."

Can you confuse your kinesthesis? Extend your arms in front of you and cross your wrists with the palms of your hands facing each other. Clasp your fingers so that they intertwine. Now bring your clasped hands toward your chest so that you can look down on your fingers. This is definitely a contorted position. Have a friend point (without touching) to a finger and ask you to wiggle it. You're going to have a problem figuring out which finger to move. The contorted position confuses your vision, so you don't know which finger belongs to which hand.

Your kinesthesis is not confused, however. If you close your eyes and think to yourself, "I'm going to wiggle the middle finger of my left hand," you'll instantly find your way through the puzzle.

Matters of Weight

How Randy is using KINESTHESIS to get money for a new bike...

If I guess which one has the 2 quarters, I get to keep the money, RIGHT? And then can I try to guess which envelope has a ten dollar bill and which one has a _twenty_? And can I keep the money if I guess right?

You can use kinesthesis to feel differences in weights. Do an experiment to see how. You will need three quarters, two envelopes, and a pair of shoes.

Put two quarters in one envelope and one quarter in the other envelope. Seal both envelopes. Hold an envelope in each hand. Can you tell which one has two quarters and which has only one? Test your friends and parents. Most people won't have any trouble telling which is which.

Now put an envelope in each shoe. Can you tell which shoe contains the envelope with two quarters? Not likely. The difference in weight, that of one quarter, is still the same. But each shoe weighs so much more than the envelope and the quarters that you are no longer able to tell the small difference between them.

With lots of practice you can learn to tell small differences in weight. Experienced deli workers can slice almost exactly the amount you ask for before they put it on the scale.

Pain? It's in the brain!

Too much pressure from a blow or intense heat or cold can cause pain. You feel pain when you have too much stimulation or when you are injured. An injury causes damaged cells to give off a chemical that makes your nerves fire. Pain reaches your brain through the many free nerve endings in your skin and other tissues. Pain can be a warning that there is danger, or it can make you seek the proper attention to take care of an injury. People who are born without the ability to feel physical pain need to constantly check themselves for injuries.

Pain is not well understood by scientists. Sometimes if a person is injured at a time when his life is being threatened, he will not feel any pain until he is out of danger. Later the pain tells him to take care of himself so the wound can heal. We feel pain only when painful messages reach the brain. If you are unconscious or under an anesthetic you don't feel pain because your brain is asleep. Some people can train their minds not to feel pain. Hindu swamis, for example, can walk on hot coals without burning their feet. Interestingly, there are no pain receptors in the brain itself. Brain surgery is often done under local anesthetic for the skull and scalp. The patient is awake as the surgeon cuts.

How much pain can you stand? Here's an experiment that won't injure you but will test just how tough you are. You can have a pain endurance contest with your friends. For each person, you will need a glass and a can of soda. Fill the glass with a freshly opened can of soda. Stick your tongue into the soda while someone counts off seconds (one-thousand one, one-thousand two, one-thousand three, etc.). See how long you can keep your tongue in the soda. Do some people have better pain endurance than others?

Most people can hardly last a minute. You can drink carbonated soda because you swish it around in your mouth and no one place is continually bombarded with bubbles. The reason you feel pain when you hold your tongue in the soda is because your saliva changes the carbon dioxide in the bubbles into carbonic acid. It is a weak acid that your nerves find irritating. Scientists found that when people were treated with a drug that blocked the acid-producing action by the saliva, they no longer felt the sting of the bubbles. In another experiment people drank soda in the high-pressure chambers used by deep-sea divers. Here the soda had no bubbles. But the dissolved carbon dioxide still produced the tingling sensation.

Itching and Scratching

Here's a way you can reliably produce an itch. Open a paperclip and run the pointed end very lightly over your lower lip and the skin just outside the corner of your mouth. This little irritation, particularly on the tiny downy hairs, stimulates an itchy sensation. The irritated cells give off a chemical that makes the nerves send signals to the brain that are similar to pain signals.

Hurry!

I TOLD you that stopping by the swamp would make us late, Margaret!

Scratching gets rid of most itches. It is stronger and less irritating than an itch and will block the itchy feeling. It stimulates a flow of blood to the spot. Blood can bring an immune response that can get rid of the source of the itch. This is helpful if the itch is caused by the poison from an insect bite. And, finally, if you scratch hard enough, the pain from the scratching can take your mind off the itch.

Yeah! Now we're going to be stuck sitting in the back with the fleas!

ITCH-MAKERS CONVENTION

Now... if you want to keep 'em up at night with the itching, go for these special spots... between the toes... inside the ear... on the bottom of the foot (now that's a little tricky, we lost Elmer last year to a very daring bottom-of-the-foot mission)... the ankle...

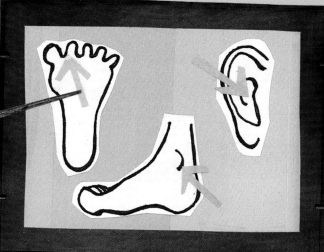

BZZZZ

BZZZ

BZZZ

BZZZZ

BZZZ

BZZZ

Tickle Talk

You can't tickle yourself. Someone else has to tickle you. When you try to tickle yourself you know exactly where you're touching yourself. You are relaxed because you are not going to be surprised. You are in complete control of the situation. When someone else tickles you, you get tense. You can't be sure where you will be touched next. Your laughter is a way of getting rid of tension.

Some people are not ticklish. They are able to stay completely relaxed. When you are being tickled, close your eyes, breathe calmly, and try to relax. Does this get rid of the tickling feeling? Before you let someone tickle you, make it clear that if you signal that you want it to stop, he or she will stop. Tickling can be cruel torture for some people.

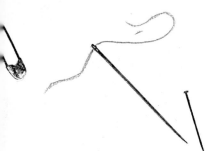

Pins and Needles

Know what happens if you sit cross-legged on the floor for a long time? Your foot falls asleep. You know the feeling—there is a prickling, tingling sensation in your foot that makes you move it around until the sensation goes away. This happens because you have squeezed some of the blood vessels and nerves that supply your foot. This cuts off the supply of oxygen and sugar to your nerves, and messages from the foot can't travel normally to the brain. Some nerves that are starved or pinched or both stop firing, while other nerves fire too much. Your brain interprets the message as a prickling or tingling sensation. It tells you to change your position.

This is a good thing. If blood flow and nerve messages are restricted for a long period of time, permanent damage can be done.

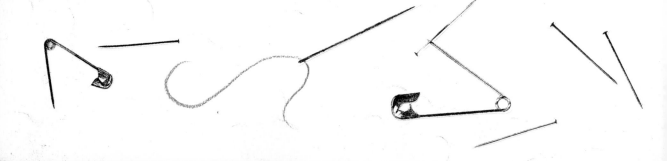

Oh, great. My foot fell asleep. Now it's not going to be able to get to sleep at my regular bedtime. It's going to be bouncing all over the bed until midnight!
ZZZZZ
door keeps
ace to store
up to ten
ng glass rack
a clever slidin

Helen Keller (1880-1968) made the sense of touch famous. She had lost her sight and hearing when she was eighteen months old. Touch became her most important sense for connecting with other people. She truly felt her way in the world. Helen Keller learned to use her sense of touch to communicate with others and to read. She learned to read speech by putting her thumb across the center of a person's lips with her fingers fanned out over the face and the back of the pinky against the voice box.